FRENCH BULLDOGS

FAVORITE DOG BREEDS

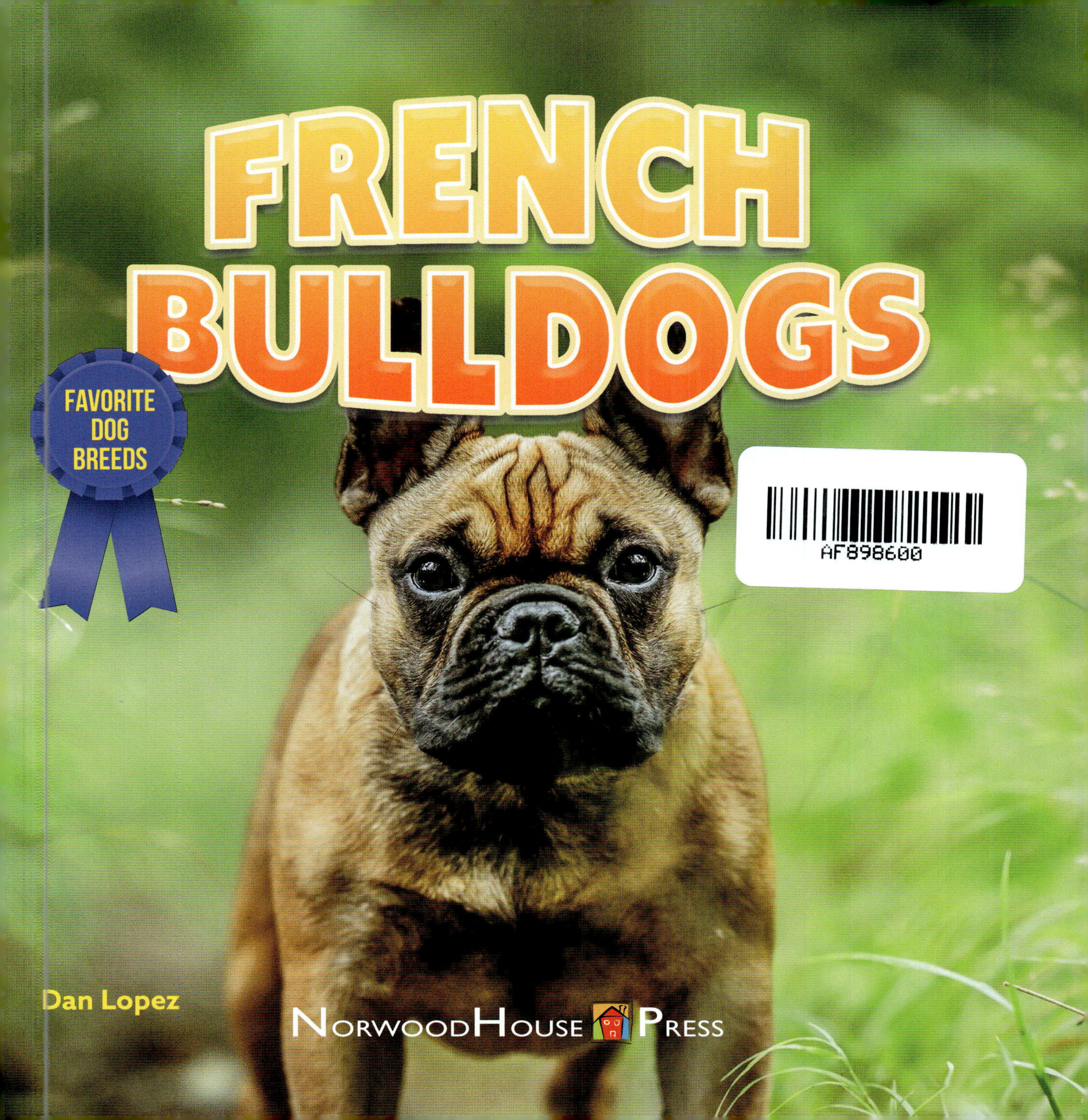

Dan Lopez

NorwoodHouse Press

Cataloging-in-Publication Data

Names: Lopez, Dan.
Title: French bulldogs / Dan Lopez.
Description: Buffalo, NY : Norwood House Press, 2027. | Series: Favorite dog breeds | Includes glossary and index.
Identifiers: ISBN 9781978580237 (pbk.) | ISBN 9781978580244 (library bound) | ISBN 9781978580251 (ebook)
Subjects: LCSH: French bulldog--Juvenile literature. | Dog breeds--Juvenile literature.
Classification: LCC SF429.F8 L67 2027 | DDC 636.72--dc23

Published in 2027 by
Norwood House Press
2544 Clinton Street
Buffalo, NY 14224

Designer: Rhea Magaro
Editor: Tricia Hoffman

Photo credits: Cover, p.1 gruzova.photo/Shutterstock.com; p.4 Sbolotova/Shutterstock.com; pp.5, 10, 11 Wikipedia; p.7 Francine parent/Shutterstock.com; p.8 Nynke van Holten/Shutterstock.com; p.9 George Trumpeter/Shutterstock.com; p.13 Julian Sarmiento/Shutterstock.com; p.14 9919/Shutterstock.com; p.15 Hollysdogs/Shutterstock.com; p.16 yhelfman/Shutterstock.com; p.17 Belavusava Alena/Shutterstock.com; p.18 Firn/Shutterstock.com; p.19 everydoghasastory/Shutterstock.com; p.21 Margarita Mindebaeva/Shutterstock.com

Printed in the United States of America

TABLE OF CONTENTS

Meet the French Bulldog

French bulldogs, or Frenchies, are popular pets. Dogs of this **breed** are known for being cute and friendly and having large, bat-like ears.

The famous French artist Henri de Toulouse-Lautrec painted a Frenchie named Bouboule.

What Do French Bulldogs Look Like?

French bulldogs look like English bulldogs shrunk down to a **miniature** size. Frenchies stand up to 13 inches (33 centimeters) tall. They weigh up to 28 pounds (13 kilograms).

A Frenchie has a square head with a short nose. Its face is covered in heavy wrinkles.

These dogs have short, smooth **coats** that come in different colors. Some are white, golden brown, or **brindle**.

Where Do French Bulldogs Come From?

As they sewed, lace makers in England held little bulldogs on their laps. In the 1850s, machines took over their work. Many moved to France with their dogs.

The dogs became **fashionable**. People all over France wanted them as pets. They were called *Bouledogue Francais*.

Today, people around the world love French bulldogs. They are at the top of the list of the most popular dogs in America.

Some Frenchies are social media stars!

Do French Bulldogs Make Good Pets?

Frenchies make great **companions**. These little dogs can live in small city apartments. They are **affectionate** and like to sit in laps.

They make friends easily with new people and with other dogs.

Frenchies do not bark a lot, but they are alert. They make good **watchdogs**.

Sometimes, they are **stubborn**!

What Do French Bulldogs Need?

French bulldogs love to play, but they do not need a lot of exercise. They should not eat too much food.

Frenchies dislike hot weather. Because they have short noses, **panting** does not cool them down very well.

These dogs need baths often. Their wrinkles need special care. A Frenchie's face should be cleaned at least once a week.

Glossary

affectionate (uh-FEK-shuh-nit): loving and caring

breed (breed): one type or kind of an animal

brindle (BRIN-duhl): brown or tan with dark flecks or streaks

coats (kohts): the hair or fur that covers animals' bodies

companions (kuhm-PAN-yuhnz): friends, buddies, or partners

fashionable (FASH-uh-nuh-buhl): liked and admired by many people; in fashion

miniature (MIN-ee-uh-chur): much smaller than the usual size

panting (PAN-ting): breathing quickly and loudly; dogs pant to bring down their body temperature

stubborn (STUHB-urn): not willing to give in or change; set on having your own way

watchdogs (WAHCH-dawgs): dogs kept to guard property

Thinking Questions

1. Describe a Frenchie's ears.
2. What colors can a French bulldog be?
3. How did Frenchies come to France?
4. Why are French bulldogs popular pets for people who live in cities?
5. Why do Frenchies dislike hot temperatures?

Index

About the Author

Dan Lopez is a writer who loves dogs! He has a German shepherd named Hans and an Irish setter named Tam. They love to go for walks in the woods together. Sometimes, they jump in the lake for a swim. Dan lives in Indiana with his wife and three kids.